DISCOVERING THE UNITED STATES

Pennsylvania

BY GEORGE ANTHONY KULZ

Kids Core
An Imprint of Abdo Publishing
abdobooks.com

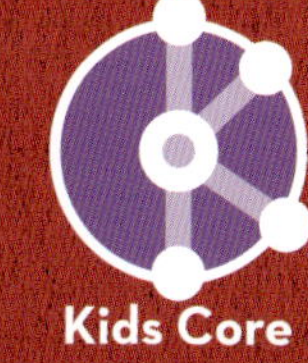

abdobooks.com

Published by Abdo Publishing, a division of ABDO, PO Box 398166, Minneapolis, Minnesota 55439.

Printed in China.
052024
092024

THIS BOOK CONTAINS RECYCLED MATERIALS

Cover Photo: Shutterstock Images
Interior Photos: MPI/Archive Photos/Getty Images, 4–5; Shutterstock Images, 7, 9 (top left), 9 (bottom left), 20–21, 28 (Philadelphia); Michael P. Gadomski/Science Source, 9 (top right); Tom Reichner/Shutterstock Images, 9 (bottom right); Andrej Safaric/Shutterstock Images, 10; Stock Montage/Archive Photos/Getty Images, 12–13; Lisa Lake/TAS23/Getty Images Entertainment/Getty Images, 15; Jeff Swensen/Getty Images News/Getty Images, 17; Heritage Images/Hulton Archive/Getty Images, 18; John Greim/LightRocket/Getty Images, 22; Sean Pavone/Shutterstock Images, 25; Mihai Andritoiu/Shutterstock Images, 26; Red Line Editorial, 28 (map), 29; Amy Lutz/Shutterstock Images, 28 (Hersheypark); Delmas Lehman/Shutterstock Images, 28 (Valley Forge)

Editor: Marley Richmond
Series Designer: Katharine Hale

Library of Congress Control Number: 2023949368

Publisher's Cataloging-in-Publication Data

Names: Kulz, George Anthony, author.
Title: Pennsylvania / by George Anthony Kulz
Description: Minneapolis, Minnesota: Abdo Publishing, 2025 | Series: Discovering the United States | Includes online resources and index.
Identifiers: ISBN 9781098294083 (lib. bdg.) | ISBN 9798384913351 (ebook)
Subjects: LCSH: U.S. states--Juvenile literature. | Pennsylvania--History--Juvenile literature. | Northeastern States--Juvenile literature. | Physical geography--United States--Juvenile literature.
Classification: DDC 973--dc23

All population data taken from:
"Estimates of Population by Sex, Race, and Hispanic Origin: April 1, 2020 to July 1, 2022." *US Census Bureau, Population Division*, June 2023, census.gov.

CONTENTS

Many important moments in US history happened at the Pennsylvania State House.

Welcome to Pennsylvania

The year is 1776. The future founding fathers gather in the Pennsylvania State House. The American **colonies** have had enough of England's strict rules. England does not allow the colonies to help make decisions.

The colonists are in the middle of the Revolutionary War (1775–1783). They are fighting for independence.

In the State House, the founding fathers **draft** the Declaration of Independence. On July 4, 1776, the Declaration is approved. The United States of America is officially born!

People can still visit this building in Philadelphia, Pennsylvania. It is now called Independence Hall. The Declaration of

The Keystone State

Pennsylvania is known as the Keystone State. A keystone is the center stone in an arch. Pennsylvania is the middle state of the original thirteen colonies. It also played a key role in the start of the United States.

Pennsylvania's state motto is "virtue, liberty, and independence." This motto can be seen on the state's flag.

Independence was written and signed there. The US Constitution was also drafted there. Independence Hall is one of the many amazing treasures Pennsylvania has to offer.

Key Facts about Pennsylvania

Pennsylvania is in the Northeast region of the United States. It borders six other states. New Jersey is to the east. New York is to the north. West Virginia, Maryland, and Delaware are to the south. Ohio is to the west.

There are six major land areas in Pennsylvania. The Atlantic Coastal Plain is mostly flat and low. The Piedmont **Province** contains forests and fields used for farming. The New England Province has many steep hills and ridges. There are thick forests in the Appalachian Plateaus Province. The Central Lowland Province has low ridges. These were

Pennsylvania Facts

DATE OF STATEHOOD
December 12, 1787

CAPITAL
Harrisburg

POPULATION
12,972,008

AREA
46,054 square miles
(119,279 sq km)

STATE BIRD

Ruffed grouse

STATE TREE

Eastern hemlock

STATE FLOWER

Mountain laurel

STATE ANIMAL

White-tailed deer

Each US state has a different population, size, and capital city. States also have state symbols.

created by **glaciers**. A large section of the Appalachian Mountain Range is in the Valley and Ridge Province.

Snow often falls in Pennsylvania from December until March or April.

Climate of Pennsylvania

Pennsylvania has a **humid** climate. It has four seasons. High temperatures can reach between 90 and 100 degrees Fahrenheit (32.2–37.8°C).

Winter temperatures can be as low as 0 degrees Fahrenheit (−17.8°C).

Atlantic Ocean storms affect the state. Storms also come from nearby Lake Erie. Pennsylvania gets more rain than many other states in the nation. Parts of the state are also very snowy.

Explore Online

Visit the website below. What new information did you learn about Pennsylvania that wasn't in Chapter One?

Pennsylvania

abdocorelibrary.com/discovering-pennsylvania

Some Europeans bought land from the Lenape people. This land became part of Pennsylvania.

The People of Pennsylvania

Two main American Indian peoples lived in this area for thousands of years. The Lenape were **nomadic**. They were fishers, hunters, and farmers. The Susquehannock traveled along the Susquehanna River. They were fur traders.

European **settlers** bought land from the Lenape and Susquehannock peoples. Later, settlers forced them to leave. Today, there are no federally recognized tribes in Pennsylvania.

Pennsylvanians Today

Almost 13 million people live in Pennsylvania today. About 75 percent of Pennsylvanians

Taylor Swift

Singer-songwriter Taylor Swift was born in West Reading, Pennsylvania. One of her first performances was singing the National Anthem at a Philadelphia 76ers basketball game. She was 12 years old. Since then, Swift has gone on to become one of the most famous singers in the world.

In 2023, Taylor Swift performed in Philadelphia, Pennsylvania. The concert was part of The Eras Tour.

are white. About 12 percent are Black. More than 8 percent are Hispanic or Latino. Four percent are Asian. Less than 1 percent are American Indian.

This state is home to the Pennsylvania Dutch people. The Amish make up part of this population. Amish people are well-known for their plain clothing and their simple way of living. They don't use much modern technology.

Culture of Pennsylvania

One of the most well-known cultural events in Pennsylvania is Groundhog Day. On February 2, people gather to see if a groundhog sees his shadow. If he does, people believe that there will be six more weeks of winter.

Different cultures have brought unique foods to Pennsylvania. Scrapple is a Pennsylvania Dutch dish. It is made from ground pork and often served with eggs and potatoes.

The groundhog used for Groundhog Day is named Punxsutawney (pronounced punks-uh-TAW-nee) Phil.

Philadelphia is known for the famous Philly cheesesteak. It was created by an Italian American in 1930.

Pennsylvania Hospital opened in 1751. It was the first hospital in the United States.

Businesses in Pennsylvania

Pennsylvanians work in many industries. The state is the largest producer of coal in the nation. Many Pennsylvanians also work in broadcasting, communications, construction, and food production.

Pennsylvania is also well-known for its history with heath care. The first **paramedics** worked there. Freedom House was a group of Black men from Pittsburgh. Their original job was to deliver food to Black people in need. But the city needed more help. The men learned how to treat some medical emergencies. They became paramedics.

Further Evidence

Look at the website below. Does it give any new evidence to support Chapter Two?

Groundhog Day

abdocorelibrary.com/discovering-pennsylvania

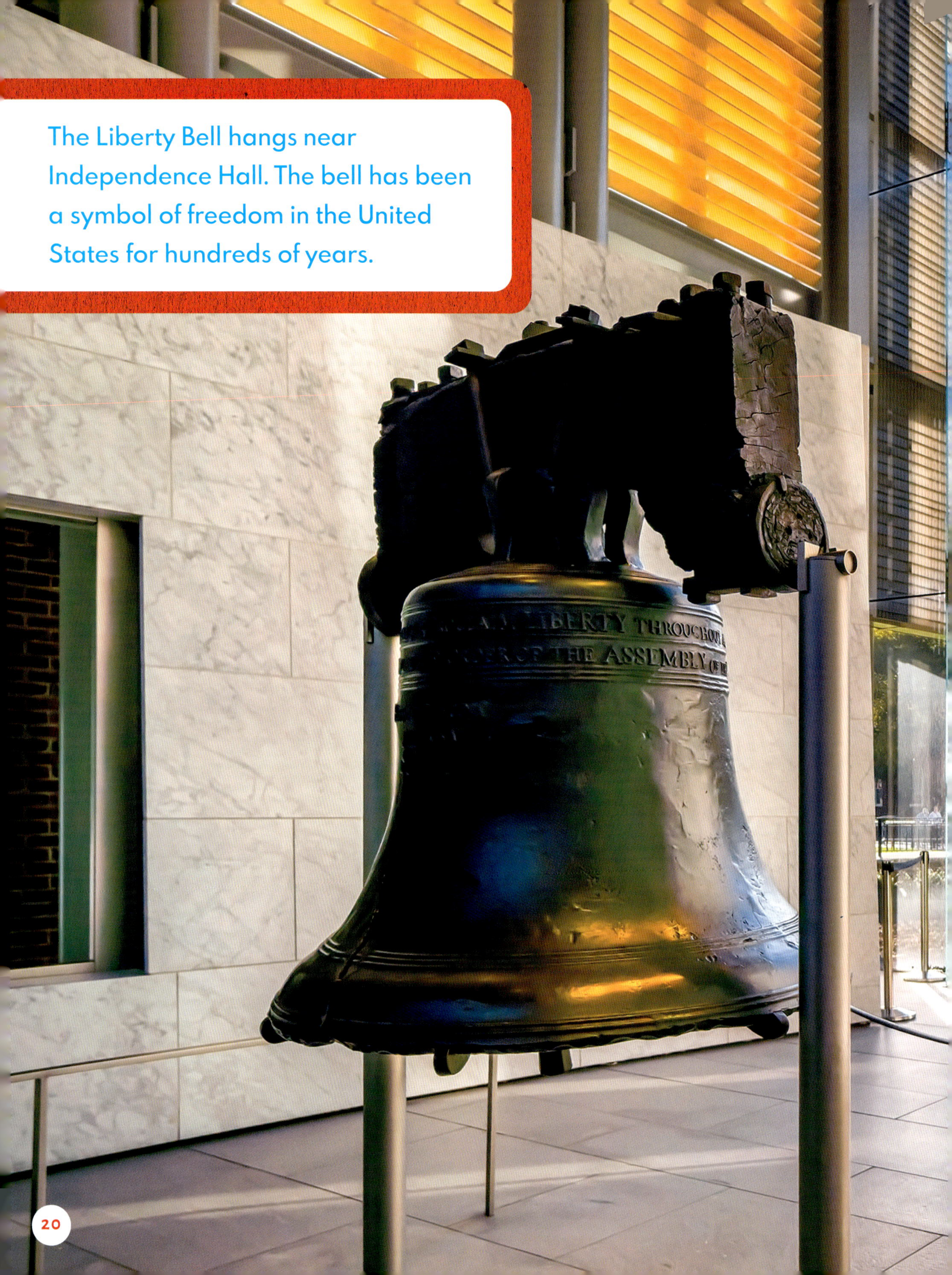

The Liberty Bell hangs near Independence Hall. The bell has been a symbol of freedom in the United States for hundreds of years.

CHAPTER 3

Places in Pennsylvania

Pennsylvania cities are rich in history. They are also home to important landmarks. The state has beautiful natural attractions too. There are many fun and popular places for people to visit in Pennsylvania.

The Franklin Institute is one of Philadelphia's science museums. The museum has a statue of Benjamin Franklin.

Historical Landmarks

Gettysburg, Pennsylvania, is the site of the largest battle in the American Civil War (1861–1865). President Abraham Lincoln gave his inspirational Gettysburg Address there. Valley Forge, Pennsylvania, is where George Washington trained his army during the Revolutionary War.

The Benjamin Franklin Museum is in Philadelphia. Franklin helped draft and sign the Declaration of Independence. The museum talks about his many inventions and discoveries. Visitors to Philadelphia can also see the President's House. Two US presidents lived there. They were George Washington and John Adams. The Liberty Bell hangs nearby.

Popular Places to Visit

There are many other interesting places to visit in Pennsylvania. The Philadelphia Zoo is the United States' oldest zoo. The Strasburg Railroad is the oldest running railroad line in the United States.

Natural attractions in the state include Lake Erie and Penn's Cave. Lake Erie is one of the five Great Lakes in North America. People can go fishing, swimming, and hiking there. Penn's Cave is an all-water cave. That means people can explore it only by boat.

Hershey, Pennsylvania, is the home of the largest chocolate company in North America.

Strange and Unusual Attractions

Every state has its share of interesting roadside attractions. Pennsylvania is no exception. The Pizza Brain in Philadelphia is the world's first and largest pizza museum. The Haines Shoe House is a five-story building shaped like a boot.

Erie, Pennsylvania, is a town on the edge of Lake Erie.

Attractions there celebrate Milton S. Hershey's chocolate company. Hersheypark contains an amusement park, shopping, and live entertainment.

Visitors can see the Pennsylvania State Capitol in Harrisburg.

Pennsylvania visitors can learn about the state's role in early US history. They can also try Pennsylvania Dutch food or visit beautiful natural locations. There is something for everyone in the Keystone State.

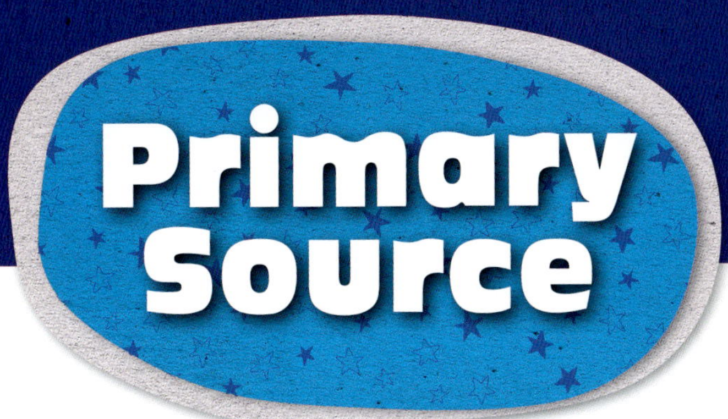

The Philadelphia Visitor Center states the importance of Independence Hall. It says:

> In this building, the Declaration of Independence and US Constitution were both debated and signed. The legacy of the nation's founding documents . . . has influenced lawmakers around the world.

Source: "Independence Hall." *Philadelphia Visitor Center Corporation*, n.d., phlvisitorcenter.com. Accessed 30 Aug. 2023.

Point of View

What is the author's point of view on this topic? What is your point of view? Write a short essay about how they are similar and different.

State Map

Hersheypark

Valley Forge National Historical Park

KEY

Capital | Park

City or town | Point of interest

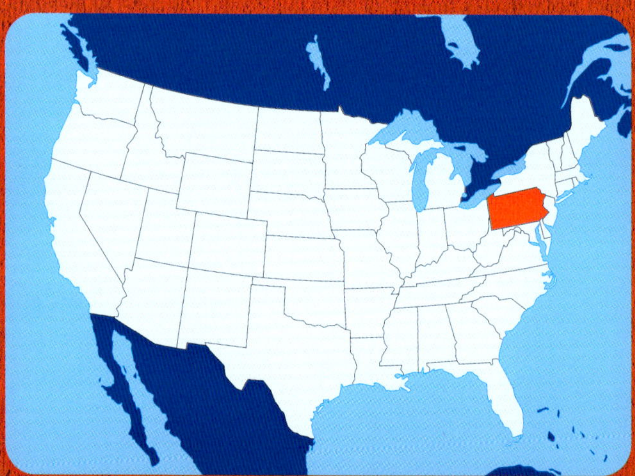

Philadelphia

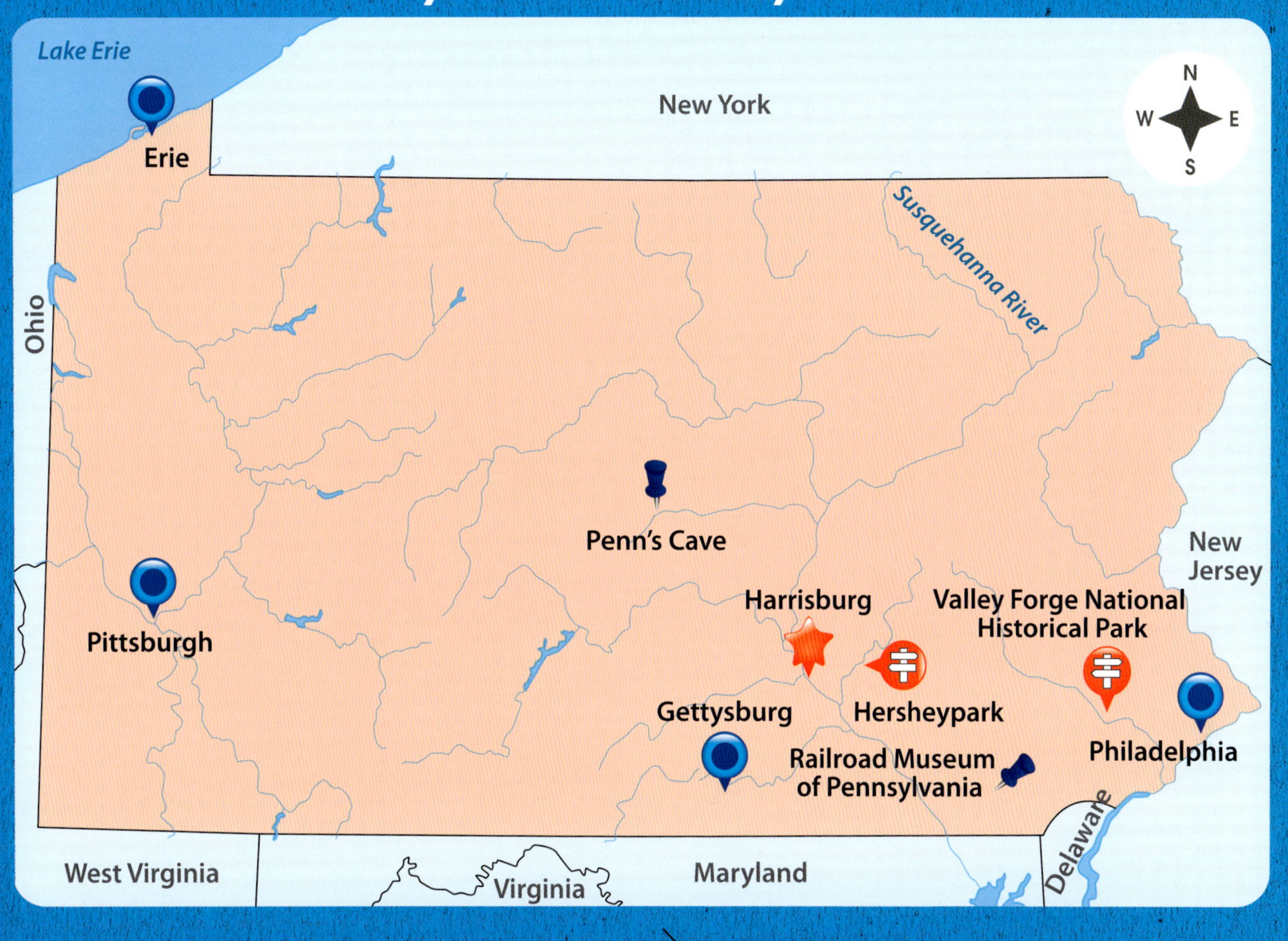
Pennsylvania: The Keystone State
Lake Erie
Erie
New York
N
W
E
S
Susquehanna River
Ohio
Penn's Cave
New Jersey
Harrisburg
Valley Forge National Historical Park
Pittsburgh
Gettysburg
Hersheypark
Railroad Museum of Pennsylvania
Philadelphia
Delaware
West Virginia
Virginia
Maryland

Glossary

colonies
areas that are controlled by another country

draft
to write an early version of a document

glaciers
masses of ice that move slowly over land

humid
describing air that has a lot of moisture

nomadic
relating to people who move from place to place

paramedics
people trained to give medical help to others outside of a hospital

province
an area of land that is defined by having common features

settlers
people who moved to a new area

Online Resources

To learn more about Pennsylvania, visit our free resource websites below.

Visit **abdocorelibrary.com** or scan this QR code for free Common Core resources for teachers and students, including vetted activities, multimedia, and booklinks, for deeper subject comprehension.

Visit **abdobooklinks.com** or scan this QR code for free additional online weblinks for further learning. These links are routinely monitored and updated to provide the most current information available.

Learn More

Miller, Karen Emily. *The Ghostly Tales of Southwest Pennsylvania.* Arcadia, 2022.

Tieck, Sarah. *Pennsylvania.* Abdo, 2020.

Index

About the Author

George Anthony Kulz is a member of the Society of Children's Book Writers and Illustrators. He writes for children and adults. In his free time, he enjoys hiking, traveling, and spending time with his family.